T0369512

For Those Who Seek To Know

The Poetry of Soup, Book I

By
Will 'is Stevens

Order this book online at www.trafford.com
or email orders@trafford.com

Most Trafford titles are also available at major online book retailers.

Printed in the United States of America.

ISBN: 978-1-4269-6759-7 (sc)
ISBN: 978-1-4269-6758-0 (e)

Trafford rev. 05/03/2011

www.trafford.com

North America & international
toll-free: 1 888 232 4444 (USA & Canada)
phone: 250 383 6864 ♦ fax: 812 355 4082

Thank you for your support
Poetrysoup.com and its member poets

Table of Content

Introduction   **Page ix**

Chapter 1   Clarifying   **Page 1**

An Ode To The People-For Civility's Rebirth-The Multiplying Of The Free- Of Histories Repeat-The Steering Of The Course-A Time of Change- All Words Of Attest- Says You Hold The Key- The Crying Voice- The Line In The Stand- There Is Coming Of A Season- An Option There Yet May Be- A Cry For Humanities Fall- Our Outrage Grows- The Crusade- An Arming Of A People- The Circling Of Vultures- The Summoning Of The Three- What Was One Is Now Two- The Act Of Repealing- Taking Your Lumps- Radicals And Rebels- Against The People Will- What He Will Not Allow- Wanting No Czar-You and Your Arrogance- Do Your Feel Something In The Air

Chapter 2   Life's   **Page 35**

Are Life's Tips- Features Of The Heart- Knowing- I Speak In A Tongue- Why Wait- Being Forced- The Unseen Cut- A Truth Of Love- A Child- Smiles Of A Daughter- A Son's Hug- Possession By Her- Trusting- Feelings Of Love- I Desire So- Poetry- Unbridled Passion- A Man's- Going Into The Night- Even Fear- In Friendship- Missing You- Your Will- My Velvet Stain- Truths Gift- An Ode To You- Thus Fallen- Father And Child- Father- The Heart

Chapter 3   Understanding of   **Page 65**

Liberty Is-The Power of Belief- Between Darkness and Light -The Coming Of Brighter Days- The Pain and Joy Of Sex- Clicks-Despots All-The Enigma- -Stating What Union -Honoring The One – Requires Sighting- The Paths And The Planks- Desires And Wills

Chapter 4   Everlasting   **Page 81**

The Poetry of Soup-For You- I –Myself-Me- Yours- Mind- His-
Communicating Intelligently –Home-Creativity- Health-Balance-
Regeneration- Mental Explorations – Work On- Wishes- Undoing- The
Pattern-The Repealing Of An Act- Yielding- The Roaring of A Lune-
Knocking and Asking- Flawed Yet I Stand –Inspiration –The Blue Marble's-
Past, Present, And Future

Chapter 5   Spiritual   **Page 109**

Zephyrs-Evokers-Irrigators-Dry Landers-Embracing- Forever-I AM –Love
–They Who Watch –Never Quit- Always- Worship- Only Death –He
–Who –Eternal –Etheric Vibrations Are- Heavenly Fathers'-Those Who
Seek To Know-Revolving life-Force – Omnipotent All Encompassing- For
Universal and Harmonious – Sacrificing Of – Ultimate – Savior- Emissary
-Join Thee

Chapter 6   Truths   **Page 137**

Now And Forever- Inscribers- Enunciated – Righteous-Eternity –Having
Of A Vision Or Dreaming- Everyone Of Ye- Learning To Love-Good Is
– God Says –Union-Regardless of –Thee –Souls -All

**Epilogue   Clarifying Life's
Understanding Of Spiritual Truths**   **Page 157**

Resources   **Page 164**

Introduction

The Traveler

Setting one upon a path
The beginning of knowledge is based in math

Yet we move forward so fast
Failing to understand yet our past

A brilliance of light
A clearness of sight

Through the vastness of what's called space
It is how He comes here to this place

Coming from a far
Way beyond distant Star

Some may call him the Unraveler
Few will call him the Traveler

The One

Speak only of love
For he is eternal
Mercy upon me
I am your servant

Father

I know it is not I,
It is the Spirit of the Father,
Who gives life,
Power and action,
Through the impulse,
Of my thoughts,

Changing of circumstance,
Requires movement,
Otherwise there can be no improvement,

Affecting every single second that follows,
Is a matter of choice,

The hopes and fears of everyone,
Are inside each us,

Ultimately,
Within the Spirit,
Lies the means to any end

Chapter I

CLARIFYING

An Ode To The People

A crushing defeat to humanity
A hidden victory to insanity

Where patriots are sure to die
Where tyrants believe they can fly

The full truth remains unseen
By those whose thoughts are unclean

The lead us as lambs to the slaughter
Having forgot the word of our father
All life they willingly barter
As they maul the falling dollar

Deceive yourself no more with their lies
For we all must stand now with one cry
Or our land will surely die

The time for justice is at hand
No longer can we withstand
The shackles placed on us by man

While they rob you and me
What we have by our own decree
Our liberty and right to be free

I tell you now of this theft
Before it leads us all to our deaths

So please do not be mistaken
The time is now to awaken
The future is ours for the taking

United together we are unequaled
Let us decided as a people
For we all are unique yet equal

For Civility's Rebirth

We have none to spare
Words they sometimes scare
It is with words I do dare
This is war they have declared

Has it always been our fate?
The entering this state
While it is never to late
Fear still turns to hate

He who believes he more sophisticated
Thinking he is most obligated
Keeping the people subjugated
Which is to be eradicated?

Pretending you are not savages
While drinking your beverages
Your greed plunders and ravages
Wealth in deed has leverages

On the surface courteous
The soul treacherous
They acts lecherous
Truth virtue less

The public has its needs
Though we are not your steeds
If you continue to proceed
Some will do more than bleed

Still small in faction
Spurred into action
Expecting this reaction
Results not your satisfaction

When it comes to our affairs
We decide upon what's fair
That is those who truly care
They ones whom are destined to heir

The intent is not to be rude
Nor is it to allude
The people will no longer brood
Now comes a time we must feud

It will be done to the subliminal
The calling of the criminal
Though long-term effects will be minimal
You see, our rights are infinitely continual

You believe us mere ordinary
Yes, you have more than one canary
Yet, see how we parry
Still we remain extraordinary

Riches of seniority
Doesn't grant superiority
We are the majority
The Ultimate Authority

The dawn of a new society
The moment of sobriety
A world community
Based on unity

No longer frightened
These newly enlightened
The world's future Titans
The consciousness of the heighten

A transformation of education
Spills forth much jubilation
 Developing a new revelation
Overcome with elation

A world of human liberty
A world of purity
A world of one community
The birth of civility

The Multiplying Of The Free

People of the world why do you wait
I continue to pontificate

Though the hour grows late
We still control our fate

Let us call for a cleaning of the slate
With words not filled with hate

The time is now to rejuvenate
All minds begin to illuminate

Congregate across the land
A long side your fellow man

Ban together in stride
We now can no longer hide

Filled with a world of pride
We all walk together in stride

Our numbers indeed will be multiplied
Though some shall yet be crucified

Of Histories Repeat

Conspiracy I say is a foot
Come forth I say and look

From the words of those who have past
Their meanings will forever last
For those who hold to them fast
Cannot helped but be set to task

For if history is bound to repeat
For all their victories shall end in defeat
For the enlightened will come to meet
Having driven them underneath their feet

Rebels they have become I say
Letting nothing stand in their way
The think they are here to stay
But soon their will come a day
In time they all shall pay

The debts they have come to owe
For these are the seeds they sow
For at every turn they will find a foe
When the winds of change do blow
Tossing them to and fro
Taking what they brought in tow
Whilst leaving us, here to grow

The Steering Of The Course

Once basking in this light
Feelings spur one to fight
Reasons why He palpates some to write
Daringly some do right

Spelled in the pages one stains
Words may appear to be vain
Words may they lead one to attain
The true nature of His almighty reign

Reason spiritually placed in rhyme
How many do spend their time
Composing His word in Chime
We all are made of thee One sublime

The opening of a door
The evening of a score
Spoken in many types of lore
Hopes that all will explore

Let this be the spark
Upon all hear His hark
The path chosen to embark
Truly plays thee part
Most shall receive deaths mark

The course has yet to be made clear
All have their choice to steer

A Time Of Change

The times they are a changing
Best start your rearranging
Cause they are a certainly changing

As if stolen by thieves
There comes the falling of leaves
As our liberty bleeds
A tree stands alone in the breeze

Calling all to be wise
Begin you all to prioritize
We all may yet claim the prize

After much comprise
There will come a sunrise
Coming to all the great prize
A world spiritually unitized

All Words Of Attest

On knowing what the future holds
One should not be sold

One has been placed upon a mission
Ultimately compelled to share some intuition

Because of multiple visions
Calling for continued divisions

Even though one wishes
Someone else do thee diss'

An incision has been made
You may call me a spade
Though it has gotten me laid

Now I digress
By trying to impress
My words mean less

So here I confess
I want out of this mess

Says You Hold The Key

They who leads us into disaster
Some may think they ye master

Some just see casters

Moving now much faster
Yes they came after

Those who are fighters
Dreaming of days brighter

Not wishing to harm
Not falling for charm
Unwillingly will disarm

Riddled amongst our leaders
Many of these deceivers
Setting to task as weavers

We are not all receiving
What they are conceiving

Like pebbles in the sand
We lie across this land

A band determined to be free
Not all stand at the tree
Let all who fail to see
We the people are the key

The Crying Voice

All accomplices in our press
All playing a part in this mess

All failing to act
All misrepresenting the facts

One you should all revere
The all forgotten, Paul Revere
Crying loud so all could hear

All the words you speak
All these words are weak

Dare tell all the true desire you seek
Dare to all make striver, you meek

We are all yet not awake
We all know it is yet not too late

Our eyes are all now glistening
Our ears are all now listening

Can you all not see, all one petitioning
Can you all not hear, all one soliciting

The Line In The Sand

Drawn is the line in the sand
Yes our time is at hand
All across this land
Tis' the hour of our final stand

From sea to shining sea
The cry of freedom calls upon thee
Standing upon feet at liberties tree
All are joined in unity

We all must pay this price
We all have thought this twice
Protectors of life's full spice
We endure and sacrifice

Rebels in power
They expect us to cower
Yet we are the tower
The real superpower

Serve a limited term
Words out of concern
Far late for you to learn
What causes us to yearn?

We have begun to awake
There is no avoiding this quake
Choose now to forsake
Choose now to remake

They will be driven out
Let their be no doubt
Hardy and stout
We will take away their clout

Dare they not see one clue?
When all began to stew
Feeling the wind as it blew
Patriots to the end this is true

Rebels acting like devils
No longer evil bed fellows
Creating civil upheavals
Using they illegal's

A cause for just backlashes
After some clashes
No longer under lashes
We rise from the ashes

Though our numbers are few
We will begin a new

There Is A Coming Of A Season

It has come to be no surprise
The lies told in disguise
Unfolding right before our eyes

As the mistrust in people grows
An army is built to dispose

From those whom we elected and trust
Now at the point of our utter disgust
They will finally reveal their true lust

No longer can we deny
Reason we must now apply

For tis' the coming of this season
For which they will call this treason

And Option There Yet May Be

Those corporate fat cats
Taking us for saps
As they toss us their scraps
Is it not the same as a slap?

Here is what I confess
Having of assess
Realize you have been blessed
The people do not depress

Treating us like bitches
Move beyond your riches
Be the one that switches
Create new stitches

Eliminate the need
Those feelings of greed
With you I plead
Plant a new seed

A Cry For Humanity

What for is this insanity
That in which grips all of humanity
Oh, for one to scream such a profanity
Recognizing all is just vanity

A true altruism of the soul
Is for one to forever remain bold
Humanity shall not remain to be so cold
A book that has yet to be foretold

The sharing of brotherly love
This true understanding of heaven above
An understanding not by force or a shove
This true friendship in which I speak of

I speak of one with compassion
Praying one day it shall be the fashion
These words I speak now with passion
Praying one day that all will ration

Sensing all shall come to embrace
In His championship we all invoke the chase
Oh, what shall we remake in its place
The true benevolence of His one true grace

A cry to all for personal veracity
Escaping all materialism with capacity
Enduring all in mind to thee tenacity
The sighting in fallacy all thee mendacity

For Humanities Fall

They listen to their own voices
While speaking of hard choices

Why have they still yet to learn
Limit their term
For all those concerned

Giving someone else a turn
Either way we will burn
All will come to rest in the urn

From lashes to ashes
From fascist who cashes

Capitalism to Socialism
Claiming humanitarianism

Our Outrage Grows

Oh, how you ignore
The People's roar
Leading us to war
This evening the score

History has shown
You should have known
Our nations no clone
Begin to hear our moan

There are those who endorse
The choosing of this course
Resorting to enforce
Starting their own remorse

A thing of mythology
Your own ideology
What is thee doxology?
This thee psychology

What gives you thee right?
As they scheme at night
Believing they have might
As they continue to rewrite

Making their commands
Overlooking our demands
Power always will change hands
All do stand to understand

Stop greasing your palm
Starting reading your psalm
Keep the country calm
Pilot away from harm

This path they chose
Here the words I compose
The public now knows
Our outrage out grows

The Crusade

Before the next decade fades
Their will bring a crusade
Befalling many by the blade
By many way of getting paid

The coming of this coup
Some will say it is well over due
Spinning in words to you
Here is yet another view

All trying to attain
Each fighting in-vain
All trying to rule this domain
So what of this reign?

There has been enough tattle
Have all not heard the rattle
Not all agreed, united by prattle
All shall bear witness, to slaughtering cattle

Will of all thee thy new decree
The answer for all in each you see
Victory in He who hears thy plea
Victory in He who determines dies free

An Arming Of A People

Post script for all oppression
The answering for all transgression
Abandoning all discretion
Causing to all a secession

They start by robbing the stores
Tools needed for their chores
A breaking down of doors
One does not hear if he snores

Words what do they mean
All have yet not scene
All have yet to see the smokescreen
Most still continue their routine

Advancing upon all is reform
Going beyond all the norm
The efforts to all must transform
The conclusion to all in this storm

In truth to all is scarred
In truth some will is to be charred
In truth no matter how hard
In truth we all stand as guard

The Circling Of Vultures

Look up to the sky
See them as they fly
Soaring not so high
You can look them in the eye

The heavens become black
Behold how they ransack
We are just a snack
Here comes the attack

They set the world a blaze
Feeding in a craze
Changing our ways
This is how it plays

Traitors to the cause
They made their own laws
Filling their claws
Without even a pause

Before you fill with dread
Know you they are dead
The sickness has spread
A tough road lies ahead

It will soon be clear
They are setting up a new sphere
As you drink your beer
They sneak in your ear

The Summoning Of The Three

How can all not agree
That the summoning of these three
Was not done by some degree
By a few others earlier decree

Washington away they go
The truth they scream to know
Prove to us that you don't owe
Prove to us that you are not a foe

All understand how they feel
All our suppose to heal
All have a choice to turn the wheel
All results in death's or life's seal

Better to stand with He
All united at His tree
Even if all shall lose both knee
All shall in deed be free

Life, will does so command
All have individual demand
Every thing does not always go as planned
All do not receive His brand

What Was Once One Is Now Two

A dichotomy in all has been born
Not created by all in scorn
None the less, all are torn

A country all divided in apart
A bounty of all the words of depart
A foundry of well made tarts

The signal to all they debase
Through the card they call race
The freedom of all they shall erase

A bipartisanship for all to divide
A partisanship setting all to collide
A relationship to all effecting worldwide

The Act Of Repealing

As the People speak of revoking
They begin their invoking
Later the land begins its smoking
They must have thought we all were joking

What they have chosen to enact
Forcing We the People to react
Even though the deck has been stacked
We the People's will withstand thee attack

How will those who gaffer defend
Against all who are bound to contend
Our will they no longer shall amend
The choice of all is their will to extend

By our own executive order
We all shall enter disorder
Taking the world to the border
This their attempting to reorder

Believing they alone are valid
Speaking amazingly in ballad
While we all scream invalid
Their address is nothing but pallid

Do not speak of un-repeal ability
We know the legit ability
Responding with hostility
Having lost their senility

Taking Your Lumps

I had a hunch
Taking us for chumps
You look rather plump
For stealing my lunch

You created this bill
Yea a poison pill
One meant to kill
For your bank bill

If your health is quite well
Then you won't go to jail
If it should fail
Then your coffin they will nail

Those that had served
You really had the nerve
Soon you will observe
The strength of our reserve

Your are the ones that dumps
Thinking he trumps
We are the ones who bumps
Leaving you with lumps

Radicals And Rebels

The iconoclast annihilate the latter
The progressives are hear to shatter
You leftist to none of thus matters
You reformers do blood spatters

Denouncing the account of what has been
Eloquently arranging your spin
Claiming there is no such sin
Signifying your intent to win

A nonbeliever who refuses to see
A developer who hacks at the tree
The instigator smiles with glee
Dogmatist denying we are free

Revisionists with their own certainty
Dividing all by our ethnicity
Partisans all bring publicity
The ringleaders to all duplicity

The demonstrator of atrocity
The subversive display there viscosity
Ultraists have of no curiosity
Heretics using your ferocity

The Insurrectionist will say its revolt
The nihilist act after receiving a jolt
Militants continue to use their bolts
The zealots sound the discharging of colts

Against The Peoples Will

Most certainly not run of the mill
Deciding can be such a thrill
Though not when it leads to kill
The executing of One's Free Will

It is one's attempt to effect
The path in life one selects
Resulting not always in what one expects
The determining in the path one thinks correct

A purpose has been carried out
From time to time we rather not tout
Per chance it leaving us not so stout
A Choosing of a particular route

On the other hand you begin to perceive
The thoughts one commences to weave
Is true they become those that one believes
Are the one's, one soul achieves

An animal of a particular kind
Is what, they would like to define
An attempt in keeping us blind
You see, we are all a part of mankind

We hail from the same community
Born, none are exempt from impunity
Yet we all possess a unique opportunity
The potential for ultimate human unity

Understanding that not one particular group
Shall stand on top of the coop
Life shall always run its particular loop
They who fail to understand shall always get the boot

An alliance that is always intact
This principle faces a constant attack
One solely meant to distract
The true history of our unique compact

The desire of the masses
Let there be no classes
All dream of greener grasses
All waiting it, as time surpasses

A waiting a certain verbification
The anointing of a new foundation
Leading all into a formation
A design of I am, He, The One of creation

Those of the determined Proletariat
Are those whom are appointed to inherit it?
All are meant to carry and assess it
All the populous are called into duty by it

What He Will Not Allow

Misters who do you think you are
Someone seemingly so bizarre
Believing they are the one unique star
All should worship from afar

With the upper hand they used as plow
Expecting us all to continue to bow
Oh to this, we all say to them now
Freedom until death, we all do vow

Executing whomever you can
Fulfilling the ultimate authoritative plan
Placing all in one grand frying pan
Enslaving thusly the world of man

It takes not a master sleuth
We all can discover this truth
We know they poison our youth
Well before they enter the booth

Many continue to ask, what shall you do
Many will move into task, when begins your coo
When all come to stand against you
Where shall your nefariousness on all spew

How will you display to all their avail
No longer covered by their veil
We all finally refuse to hail
We all no longer shall be in jail

Wanting No Czar

Even if force
Has to be a source
Resulting in much discourse
We must change this course

You to all I employ
This gives no particular joy
But I will not longer be coy

My words to thee
We will stay free
Better end your spree

Who do you think you are?
Judging from afar
Time to raise the bar
We want no czar

You And Your Arrogance

Has it become a liability?
The displacing one's credibility
Or is it a disability
One due from our own gullibility

Maybe it's just ones disdain
The reason for their particular campaign
Believe this world is not to blame
Awaking in all that they are not the same

Showing they have become negligent
By the setting of new precedents
Are they even are resident?
We can call Heaven sent

Maybe it is just pride
Being a perversion their hide
We all know it has to be their guide
Upon which they all ride

One must put it blunt
They delineate a false front
As they pull their stunt
All should see a shunt

Do You Feel Something In The Air

Something isn't quite humanly right
These conditions of humanly plight
These feelings of humanly fright
They take all humanly might

These feelings of human frustration
Causing such human sensation
Giving birth to human dedication
Be free of human domination

Having not much human time to spare
Impressions of a human only one can bare
All whom are human want none of this affair
All know what is in-human, is in the Air

It seems so humanly all clear
But yet still humanly all fear
Within the in-humanly, up coming year
Something humanly to all will appear

Chapter 2

LIFE'S

Are Life's Tips

Aspiring or retiring
From life's little trip
Here is one little tip
Enjoy each little sip

Features Of The Heart

Now in this feature
Know all are God's creatures

There may come many preachers
There may come many teachers

All sharing bits of knowledge
Why they all went to college

For wealth and for fame
Many wanted to attain

A quest that has brought many to shame
Their core of Heart to blame

Truth and wisdom a major part
They should have craved in Heart

Knowing

The desire to know
Seeking understanding
Thee drinking of knowledge
An unquenchable thirst

Having gained understanding
Once lost in darkness
Now over whelmed by its light

An addiction to one
An obsession to another
Ignorance is bliss
Knowing a burden

Welcomed by some
Feared by many
Knowing what they know
Yet still not knowing

I Speak In A Tongue

I speak in a tongue
Unfamiliar to some

My words have no meaning
Amongst those who are dreaming

My words hold no anger
Only to a stranger

My words hold nourishment
All those in punishment

My words come clean
Those of you who have seen

They are right before your eye
Do not sit and let them go bye

Why Wait

Waiting for truth, waiting for love
For one who denies, for one so clear
What is the glory? What is the purpose?
What once was one, has now become two
Remaining as one, forever never existed
They are two, unknown to themselves
What they have known
Barred for a time, unable to see
Living as two
Leaves one's cup half full
A soul half drained
Though joyous in thought
A nightmare to live

Reunited as one
A world awaits rule
None shall divide

So, why wait?

Being Forced

Without rhyme or reason
With cause and blame

An undeniable truth
We must face our shame

Taking away the will
Binding it in chains

Taking away our strength
The energy of the soul

The mind now blank
As we though we walk a plank

Struggling for breath
Battling with death

Having no choice
Desire is a force

The Unseen Cut

This pain in the heart
Oh, when did this start

Falling for another
Leads one to discover

So many emotions
Where is devotion?

Looking down to see a dagger
Now one begins to swagger

Feelings of betrayal
Was all a portrayal?

Here comes strife
There is no knife

Failing to have a clue
Love felt by one was true

One heart is bleeding
Nor shall it forever be receding

A Truth Of Love

Love honors, it lies
Loves gives, it denies
Love creates, but yet destroys

Before Cupid's arrow strikes
Love captures soul, mind and body
A beating heart
Bursts blood of passion

Conquering all the same
Rushing through each vein
A quickening of pulse
A shortening of breath

Oh, how I must confess

A truth of love
I dare not protest

A Child

So courageous and bold
For one not so old
Oh, how should we mold

With bravery of heart
Ah, what a good start

Feeble and kind
An Impressionable little mind

With a joy so contagious
Never cease to amazes

Stand tall and firm
In deeds so you may earn
All that is to learn

Smile Of A Daughter

A break in the clouds
Crying out loud
Claiming to declare
By these tears I do swear

The Sun in a morning sky
It is her I do spy
I did not know she could fly

A true blossoming rose
Yet, such a cute little nose
Leaving a man froze
Hope ye never close

Here comes the moon
Oh, why so soon

Beholding their brightness
Resembling her likeness

A Sons Hug

What is this I feel?
Little arms of steel

They grip so tight
Dare not one to fight

Father and Son
Truly He has begun
An attempt to become one

Possession By Her

From cradle to grave
Knowing what she gave
Who would want to save?

Denying all logic and reason
Entering this sick season

Her fragrance and grace
Still wished upon my face

Her evil desires
Only fuel to the fires

Trusting

Trusting in another
Trusting in one's self

Trusting of faith
Trusting of belief
Trust of both

Fearing what may be lost
Trusting no matter the cost

Whom trust is given
Thru whom fate is driven

Feelings Of Love

Some they come
Some they go

Others keep locked in vault
Though not entirely their fault

Feelings can be dangerous
Contemptuous and ruthless

Loves a feeling of passion
Mistaken sometimes for compassion

Feelings of love
Feelings of desire

They both spark a fire
In those whom conspire

I Desire So

Thee my dear lass

Know this all shall pass
After coming so fast
Though this night shall not last

And one should not fuss
Over such a permanent lust

Passions have driven
Forever forbidden
They are no longer kept hidden

As it comes, so it goes
Starting not at my toes

The battle begins
Fearing without end

Knowing that you know
How much, I desire you so

Poetry

Oh, what do I know of thee
Oh, how you flow out of me

How much time will pass?
How long will this last

The words they come so fast
Appearing in a flash

Turning me around
Before knocking me down

Oh, He why poetry?
What do I know of...He?

Unbridled Passion

Unbridled passion
Meant for more than one session

Taking you in tow
Away we go

Basking in our fires
Oh, what the bliss of our desires

Continue to let us conspire
Always before we retire

Lust having hit its mark
All unbridled passions will spark

Let us no longer annoy
Taste enjoy

Pleasure is delicious
So sweet and suspicious

Come my muse
Having no more refuse

A Man's

I am merely a man
Doing the best I can

You judge me for my plan
Doing the best I can

So you are not a fan
Doing the best I can

Yes I look really tan
Doing the best I can

Unlike those who ran
Doing the best I can

I make my final stand
Doing the best I can

In front of him when I stand
Did the best I can

Going Into The Night

Into the night
We both take flight

Our fancy our delight
Under beautiful star light

Come this night
Here out of sight

We make a star's light
We can no longer fight

Both are right

Taking such a flight
Into this night

Even Fear

Sitting in fear
Sssh, can't you hear
An evil draws near

Confusion his friend
Chasing without end

Looking into this mirror
Feeling one is so inferior

Seeing all that is me
How could one not see?

I fear me

In Friendship

A kinship of fellow
Even though we may bellow

Words so unkind
Leaving one blind
Lost in one's mind

Love is for you
All there is to do

Become such a friend
Forgive with out end

The Missing You

Not knowing why
My thoughts make me cry

Always to stew
The of missing you

Feeling so blue
Because of missing you

Yes, all this is true
Forever missing you

Wonder if you have a clue
How I am missing you

Even today born anew
Still I be missing you

Your Will

What is it about you?
Why so blue?

What have you at hand?
Is this humanities last stand?

Swallow this if you will
Follow this at your will

Knowing one may kill

Stay your hand this day
Call upon him and pray

Live in a virtuous way

My Velvet Stain

She came in like the wind
Portraying herself a friend

Such a sharp poke in the eye
My mishap with this Gemini

She hid her flame
Having much disdain

From something so plain

Longing for change
She denies the same

This Velvet stain

Truth's Gift

Through trials and tribulations
Having known much elation

Forging ahead
Feeling much dread

A vision becomes clear
Causing much fear

Blessed with such power
One cannot go an cower

No longer to sift
You have been given a gift

Seek knowledge and understanding
They will leave you standing

Once wisdom is gained
His gift will be famed

An Ode To You

An ode to you
One so simple yet true

You hold such passion
Many find not in fashion

The desire in you
Please be true

Your face is like grace
Oh, just to keep pace

But to be behind
So fine

Oh, if I only had the time
The drinking of your wine

Even for this small a time
It would be one so Devine
Being lost in time

Thus Fallen

Many have fallen
Many felt a calling

Your purpose far greater
So says, your creator

Your lives have been cut short
Your lives are not sport

Do no evil that divides
Filling with greed and false pride

Your death be in vain
Not all fall the same

Father And Child

You try so hard
Playing each card

By denying one found
After becoming so bound

No matter how far
Even to distant star

A child love for father
Goes much farther

A father's love for child
Will tether him each mile

If you hold to this fast
Surely your love will last

The Heart

Why does my heart torment me so?
Having known love and lost

A love unkind
A love cruel

Tearing the heart
Ripping it apart

Into daggers of despair
They stab the soul with each thought

A cry of agony
The pain unbearable

Living with or without
Love has left one in doubt

Forever seeking
Forever critiquing

Love not forsaken
A heart not taken

Chapter 3

UNDERSTANDING OF

Liberty

Freedom of liberty
A curse for purity

Unbridled free will
Surely will kill

Where is the fence
That rein's arrogance
Over ran by zealousness
Evil and greed

Here is a lasso
Let justice fly
Here is a fence
Its righteousness, I cry

The Power Of Belief

Believe you sit in his right hand
Believe in one's own hand

Believe they both play a part

Belief is perception
Belief is reality

A power given to all

Shaping the present
Forming the future

He who believes
He to his own peril

Dying for one's belief
Enduring for one's everlasting life

One's belief
Power of the Almighty

Between Darkness And The Light

Dwelling in Darkness
Believing to see
A light shines brightly
Casting doubt upon thee

The darkness is cold
How long should one hold
The light truly sears
Burning away all tears

Walking in the darkness
Ignorant of truth
Walking in the light
Carries a burden of truth

Who thinks he chooses
He chooses you

The Coming Of Brighter Days

Can mere words really express?
The pain of my mind and heart's distress

Seeing the hold of his embrace
My heart fills with the shame of disgrace

My mind continues to ask why
Eternal love, surely it cannot die

Am I just refusing to see?
That this was not meant to be

Was my love really this true?
Must be why I am feeling so blue

Some day the mind and heart shall mend
There are other matters to attend

The coming of brighter days
Gives birth to many new lays

The Pain And Joy Of Sex

I believe I've had a sprain
After this one particular drain
This once spectacular strain
Has left me now in pain

Projecting this subject with respect
Still will be those who have words of object

The elegant touch of her skin
Oh God, she must be my twin
These feeling cannot be a sin
Coming as one glides within

The feel of thee electricity
The wave of thee multiplicity
Gives way to this duplicity
Sex in its simplicity

Now we are disconnected
Never again to be connected
Considering the choices one has selected
The responsibilities one have neglected

One should have stood tall and protested
All of that which is detested
Now much time must be re-invested
Courage will truly been tested

Clicks

Something has gone off in my head
Nor longer am I filled with dread
The glory of his spirit has spread
Here the words thy lord has said

You have been given a gift of sight
A glimpse of something so bright
Filling ones heart with utter delight
Speaking the grace of God's full might

Oh Lord, how am I to cleave
Let alone have them believe
Thy words I have yet to receive
They'll say I am out to deceive

Let all here my voice
All must be given a choice
Listen closely to thy own inner voice
And soon you shall rejoice

Despots All

Here the words of this responder
About those who use transponders
Thinking we can't see that far yonder
Our life's blood they wish to squander

All pointing a finger of blame
What is your particular aim?
Why are you trying to inflame
Is it our country you try to reframe?

Believing it is you whom are destined to reign
Your own reflections shows your disdain
This effort is so inhumane
For those whom you wish to retain

You are the ones whom are oppressive
Calling yourself progressive
It is you who act aggressive
In order to be regressive

Considering your jurisprudence
These are no acts of prudence
Declaring to all your issuance
Displaying to all your imprudence

The Enigma

Some may say he is hexed
Others might say he is vexed
Though maybe he is just perplexed
Scowling through sacred text

An understanding begins to stupify
It also begins to mystify
Things unable to justify
Causing one to crucify

By his crossed he has ordained
That which cannot be restrained
His spirit will forever remain
In those who stay self-contained

The Stating Of What Union

At a time where 13 withstood
All standing for righteous and good
Hoping this all is not misunderstood
This attempt to try and make good

That which was flawed from its start
Is know bleeding us all apart
These words the One now imparts
Develop your own unique martial art

Learn all are truly distinct
Easily for some to indistinct
Desire not to become extinct
Understand all are 'Holy' interlinked

What shall come of thee unification?
The One's power of omnipotent manifestation
Leading many to their own eternal damnation
Upon He the One's final translation

Honoring The One

Like looking into the Sun
Light that truly does stun
These lyrics seen by the son

My gifts granted to all they are vast
Calling unto all that they may bask
Hold in your heart my commandments to them fast

Requires Sighting

Sight begins to unfold
Wait be patient and bold
His truth shall forever be foretold
No matter by those who chose to scold

Each man deserves his fare share
Each man's words are equally fair
Understanding comes due to dis pair
My heart goes out to you in prayer

The Path And The Plank

Contrary to what you might think
One walks a path and another walks a plank
But dare do thee fall and sink
Failing to see there is a link

One attempt at verse may fail
Yet words can still compel
Heaven some shall deed excel
The rest shall in deed go to hell

Desires And Wills

These words that have been read
Those words that have been said
Leaves all feelings of dread
Those last words done said

They thus now require
The words of electronic wire
The will of your desire
Is not the desire your of will

You see the will of ones desire
Will cause one to conspire
Always something quite dire
Causing some leading to fire

Yet in others it is fear
Spewing their words that spear
The weak they intend to jeer
Once seeing things clear

Their will is no longer content
Upon one single event
Coming with wills intent
An offer that He represents

When His will is integrated
His will is indicated
Thru His words they are intimidated
Because His mind has innovated

The Desires of ones will
Comes with great thrill
These words that one's spill
Take the blue or red pill

The will of you course
The desire of will the source
Speaking no words of remorse
Desires of the will to endorse

Seeing this of matter of choice
All things comes by voice
Articulation calling to rejoice
Still praying in silent loud voice

Leads one to jubilation
The One's thoughts lead into manifestation
They also lead into temptation
Desires gifts from thee Creation

Chapter 4

EVERLASTING

The Poetry of Soup

This night grows quite late
Still I come back to state
Having new words to relate
Knowing they may defecate

Searching the memories vast inventory
Locating one peculiar quarry
Inspiring this morning glory
Giving pompous to this story

Once surfing the web for group
Clicking the link of this particular soup
Finding an articulate troop
Thusly, throwing one for a loop

Just coming to share
Some poetry one felt fair
With no intent to ensnare
Thusly, one enters this affair

Some time in deed did pass by
Few words along the way one did apply
Not being one to defy
Thusly, returning to comply

Continuing to plod
Giving glory to God
Casting out of one unique rod
Catches one exceptional cod

Wide is this gate
Lead by words that hate
The narrowness of this gate
Is one of His higher estate

The insanity of vanity
One could scream a profanity
A cry to humanity
Believe in Christianity

For You

The coy of her kiss
Makes my heart aflame
The joy I have missed
Makes my love to blame

I

Idealistically I do what I want
I speak in mind dramatically
Aggressively going daringly after
Impulsively at times affects the latter

Myself

Passionately myself
Lusting straightforward for life
My impatient energy
Impatiently lusting for life
Myself forcefulness
Full of myself vigor
Vitality of self lots

Me

Vulnerable with a child like charm
Yet fearlessly face adversity
Bright with child like charm
Confidently face adversity

Yours

Creatively we can eventually reach our goals
Thoughtful we understand others well
Being sensible we eventually reach our goals
Quietly we understand others well

His

The loyalty of his trustworthiness is undeniable
His understanding is always reliable

Understanding His agreement
Trustworthy in His vehement

Mind

Minds indulgent artistic expression
Materialistically rewards head
Insecure is minds judgment

Communicating Intelligently

Youthful free spirits
Mischievously they are playful
Versatile
Romantic free spirits they are
Nervous however during times of introspections

Intelligently
With clear communication
Adapt-ably
Yes charming and curious
Having a wide eyed wonder
They express exuberance
Talking new possibilities

Home

Both motherly generous is His upbringing
His protective internal powerful self defense
Equally tenaciously magnanimous in its fostering
Intuitively bounteous His soft heart does dispense
Sometimes naïve in the concept of this rearing
The reward of His breeding immense
Moody yet confident one learns to understand
The unique expression in His plans

Creativity

A courageous development of eccentricity
The more vibrant and radiant thee anthropocentricity
A dominating development of providence
Refulgent is the Self in prominence

Aristocratic distinguished are elitist
Authoritatively focused are they defeatist
Opinionated expressed feelings of linguist
Proud efficient in expectations it resists

Generous good lifestyle yet has trouble relaxing
These temperamental go-getter are always relapsing
Capable an unrelenting when willing to face adversity
Enlists the support of others augmenting enthusiastically

Health

Perfect its punctuality
Self-contained in Him Honestly

Balance

Peaceable and warm hearted, having diplomacy justly fair in stability
Charmingly beguiling this petty magnetic aura polished with anguish
Appealing allure, calm with deep understanding of humilities ability
Vainly pursing a pleasing appearance, unwise self serving, dispatch and abolished
Easygoing honesty found relaxed in generous refinement in convertible sensibility
Active deceitfulness, painstaking in its conniving, arrogance its creativity, betrothed ye demolished
Time wasted, causes lost, to much on plate, unbalanced imbalanced
Detailed- oriented keen observations of affections soft touch is counter-balance

Regeneration

Athletic in ones
Strong the desire to learn
Philosophical
Mind positive in thinking
Emotionally in touch

Selective steel force
Unyieldingly craves power
Optimism inspired
Self-sufficient perception
Attracts the ones desires

Candid self assured
Paranoid and neurotic
Lacks thee true intimacy
Caused raised suspicions
He master of seductions

Mental Explorations

Selective individualistic desires
Powerful demonstrative extremist
Egocentric soulful amoralist
Tenaciously eager spontaneous liars

A philosophical love of wisdom
Is optimistic friendly and gracious
Energetically eagerly pervasive
The influential love of His saintdom

Passionate yet daring
The subtle inspired fanatical
Free spirit upon a mystical healthy sabbatical
Positive thinking in thus mental preparing

Work

Work
Boring
Know-it all
Stick-in-the -mud
Acts superior
Won't quit even if should
Stubborn, has trouble relaxing
Melancholy downright depressed
Always thinking about tomorrow
Realistic responsibility
Clever with a good head for business
This determined good role model
Honest and persevering
Cautiously sensible
Quietly focused
Good listeners
Get your way
Set goals
Work

Wishes

Assertively brings creative dazzling eccentric free-thinkers genius honestly, innovatively judiciously kind, loving many new-approaches. Originally progressive, quietly refuses self-righteous takers understanding vex, wanting exploration yon zeniths

Undoing

Spirit awakens
A soothing presence
A strong cosmic link
Highly receptive
Having special gifts

Temperamental
Feel others pain
Misunderstood
Leads people on

Let off steam
Accept change
Gracefully

Psychic
Deep feelings

Undoing

The Pattern

The clock slowly turns
Imagines start to a rise
While the sun slowly burns
Will start's in crystallization

The Repealing Of An Act

Looks like this one is back
We all no however this one is whack
We know this meant to track
All those they send to the rack

They and their double dealing
We know what you plan on stealing
How bout we all try kneeling
The worlds over due for some healing

Making a real impact
Those things meant to distract
If one's will is still intact
Better ye all make one compact

This old type of circuit breaker
The soul of ye spirit taker
The Universal will of the Maker
A spirit in God's green acre

Yielding

The ones whom have been arrested
Has found themselves tested
All is in he who has requested
His will is justly manifested

Yes we truly all are free
Come and go as you plea
Caring not for thee one Trinity
Most running quickly as they flee

Chasing for possessions across this great land
Seeking not the guidance of our Creators hand
Praying that none shall be banned
Unfortunately part of the plan

True all should seek in a hurry
No longer will any have worry
Once tasting the juice of his sweet berry
See his fruit is more than just merry

The Roaring Of A Lune

Again tonight he is on the prowl
This rather peculiar yet handsome night owl
Once something has become afoul
On his face appears his scowl

Illuminating the night of our sky
Every night it seems he drives by
A new day for him is to imply
His way of saying goodbye

Knocking and Asking

When something wicked does your way come
Fear not from all that plays a part
There is nothing in life will keeps you bay from
Austere what is purple at heart

Flawed yet I Stand

The flaw is to stumble
Imperfect at times
As bending is to humble
Still mountains to climb

Inspiration

Wanting to know where you find
The rod that is inside of the mind
This is were you look for your sign
Once you have paid the fine

The requirement is that of devotion
Keeping all things in motion
Once you feel the emotion
Now you feel his promotion

Intuition comes with understanding
Once the mind starts its scanning
A seed you mind is implanting
An inexplicable perceptive recanting

Once you have reached his border
Away from all this disorder
Your mind begins its recorder
His inspiration comes in short order

The Blue Marble

Spinning alone in your space
Traveling the universe in pace
Upon beholding all of your grace
We are trapped by you in this place
What could one possibly a face
From the actually shifting of your base
Let us say you began to retrace
Would everything commence to erase?
The things we have all chosen to embrace
You have chosen to replace
Those who have chose to deface
Are those whom you chosen to efface
Those who have well prepared their brace
This world would be yours to encase

Past, Present and Future

Begetting what is prehistoric
Bringing forth that which is ancient
Thriving on what is caloric
Generating that which is radiant

A demonstration of his word
An award from the cosmos
A deliverance of his word
An introduction from the logos

Emerging from this one feeling
A perspective of the one's intent
Arising from this one flavor
A directive of the one has been sent

Chapter 5

SPIRITUAL

Zephyrs

These new approaches'
With there clear inner vision
Pioneering and candid
They are free spirits
They have deep understanding
Yes unselfish free thinkers

Many options they see
From there insightful visions
Breathes keen observations
Magnetic aura attracts many vibrations
Harmonizing new possibilities
Through selfish diplomacy

Creatively just
They clearly communicate
Sincerely and objectively
With wide eyed wonder
Open-hearted they stay composed

Evokers

Justice believe they
They getting the most out of life
Willingly they taking chances
Staying strong in their convictions
Daringly honest to many
Winning most of their battles
The spread hope speaking their mind

Seeing the rainbow
Being always strait shooters
They have energy to burn
They are good learners
Their character develops
Inspired by the bright side
These eager starters

Friendly and gracious
Having independent thinking
A Strong desire to learn
They are big thinkers
They keep their healthy vigor
Having much vitality
Expressed in charity

Irrigators

Charming and well liked
Confident self assured style
Each has a warrior's inner strength
Successful as steel is their will
In its unique self expression
Displaying their strong outer shell

Having many friends
They do learn from others
And others learn from them
A soothing presence
Knowing that one's laughter is healing
They have learned to accept change

Creative vision
Occasionally lets of steam
They all have high stamina
Yes persevering
Observant and persuasive
Delicate, yet they are firm

Dry Landers

Caringly humble
They are good in crisis
They understand others well
They show gratitude
Appreciating fine work
They stay grounded and focused

How they get there way?
Real high productivity
Never taking silly risk
Highly efficient
A down to earth inner strength
Artistically self expressed

Their accountable
Really good reasoning
They are detailed resilient
They take care of friends
As well as conscientious
Mysterious networkers they are

Embracing

The Omega Man
He bids me tell you once again
To you and all of your kin
Living dangerously
Will lead you into trouble
Scaring other people away

Repressed emotions
Is one single-mindedness
Exaggerating the truth
Manipulation
Causing you fight wrong battles
Picking everything a part

You are self-serving
Lacking true intimacy
Operating close to the edge
Ever exhaustively so
Thinking about tomorrow
Makes you then downright depressed

Your self-righteousness
Because you lead people on
Others take advantage of you
The desolate one
Or I Am the Omega
Who will you choose as your One?

Forever

Again the choices
What ever choices you make
They what hold your fate
Pray to understand wisely
Living or die forever

I AM

I
Love
I AM
Making all
You hear the Call
Get down on your knees and pray
Live his word and I am will come to save your day
You will begin to understand that this world is not for you, I AM you
belong to

.

Love

I told you that I loved you all
Remember why I died
In forgiveness for all who sinned
You have the path to win
Requiring that you look within
Once you have let guilt go
Then a new road will start to show
A new soul will start to grow
The first time that you take his hand

Wanting to feel all of his joy
You all I now employ
No longer shall my words be coy
Love your Father, ahoy?
Know you thee of his joy

They Who Watch

They
Now they know of me
What shall become of me?
Let they not touch me

Who
Attempting boo
Why do you coo?
Has there been a coup?

Watch
Better let go of your crouch
And continue to watch
So put down your scotch
Now move up a notch

Never Quit

Victory
Cost, Price
Sacrificing, Crucifying, Dying
Patience, Faith, Strong, Self
Will, Courage
Battle

Always

Always thinking of a house, car or boat
Materialism is death combined
Think and leave behind
Always thinking of each ones husband or wife
Thy loin's they burn
Think of other concerns
Always think of the Father, Son, and Holy Spirit
Free it does the spirit
Always think within

Worship

The Father
Father I love you
Jesus I love you to
Father I love all of you

The Son
Son yes love yourself
Son yes I love myself
Son yes I love everyone else

The Holy Spirit
Holy Spirit I fall
Holy Spirit I call
Holy Spirit I Stand Tall

Only Death

Speak not of love
For you are already dead
What know you of this Dove?
For the Devil thee wed

He

He

Him
from ye
way up above
look down with love
if only all did actually see
the world ultimately would be free
there are those who won't find the key
to the kingdom of the One, Lord's Majesty
you see those whom are the sons and daughters of I am
will never completely understand, the plans of He, who is I Am

Who

He quits, He stops, He turn's
The clock, The watch, The notch
Who states, Whose fate, Whose gate
You do, You grew, Or you stew

Eternal

Its intending there is no ending time line
What unceasing undeceiving distant place
Reversible waves everlasting each one
Tuning always communing lasting ageless
Incandescent fluorescent igniter light
No disruption does do corruption draw out
As alluring and assuring does broaden
Aeonian or plutonian garden

Etheric Vibrations Are

Those things you feel when you fright
Courage's Will comes when one grows
Ever always present is He who is unknown
Do give way to feelings of peace and joy
Behold creating miracles unto thee
Dare there be destruction done by your hand
Manifest in the world what have I

Heavenly Father's

Cosmos ever so vast a universe complete

Those Who Seek to Know

For those who seek to know
As one goes about one's day
Thru poems he seeks to show
Our thoughts manifest the way

Considering starting at high noon
The words one chooses to relay
Appearing to thee ever so soon
The words one has chosen to prey

As we all move thru each hour
The spirit will choose to employ
As we all move thru each power
The spirit will choose to deploy

Revolving life-force

Coursing thru thy vein
Forever will this stigma
Effecting more than brain
Behold He thy Enigma

Omnipotent All Encompassing

There is no escaping, His pan-optic
Dare one to be complete
Better hath taken on His synoptic
When Father and son meet

Universal and Harmonious

More than metropolitan
Typifying thee identical
Great ye cosmopolitan
Concerning thee ecumenical

Sacrificing Of

All that I knew is forfeit
Blood for thy spilling
Entirely I willingly forth wit
Crucifixion a ritual killing

Ultimate

Superiority of government
Lack therefore of steam
Key to the element
Father He Supreme

Savior

Look to thee Deliverer
Call upon thy redeemer
No longer shall ye shiver
Now you see his dream

Emissary

Perilous is thy mission
Which that He represents
Saying its sedition
Who creates decent

Join Thee

Oh, to thee my glee
Ye, come here sync
He has set me free
Now ye, part His link

Chapter 6

TRUTHS

Now And Forever

Now you began to understand
One of the masters plans
Willing stand forth
At once today henceforth
Never blindingly yet everlastingly
Doing so eternally
From now until evermore
Oh, Lord Creator always
Remember praise
Eternity your will partake
Vainly work to remake
Evermore will be your fate
Reaping what have you been of late?

Inscribers

Each word one does read
Memory in my mind
Harmonic vibrations have been feed
Each emotion a different rainbow of color
Talking to self inside of head
Do you want life or rather you dead
Choose you read and write instead

Enunciated

That in which one pontificates
Indeed thoughts will extricate
Through joys and difficulties
Beholden to the bearer
This balancing of the center
Rejoicing and ailing, words in spelling

Righteous

Act I

Thee morality of one's self, leaves into question the righteousness of us all.

Finances indeed do fluctuate and those who seek to know need to understand that they are likely to continue to being so. The further continuous priority of debt accumulation must fall prey to financial disorganization.

Thee formality of caution, is maintaining stability, by decisions based on information.

Our descendants gain or loss potential goes hand in hand with education, so be the well prepared. Gain a massive wealth of information.

Do not repeat same mistakes and power plays. This maybe difficult if one's emotions are not kept-under firm control.

Remember all is suspicious and/or secretive.

An age of revolution in peoples thinking has begun.
Freedom from old age restrictions gives birth to inventiveness.

Eternity

Act II

Time and space are one
Eternity is the prize
Those who stand among towers of marble
Lucky breaks come from direction of allies.
Dare cash flow mismanaged will move in opposite directions
Investing long-term should prioritize
Eternity is the prize
Through achievement it comes
Driving higher to education gives rise
Knowing what one needs is linked
Understanding to the wise
Eternity is the prize

Timeless is our sense of moral justice
Eternity is the prize
Leading to a crusade thus hypocrisy
No longer under a guise
Ethical change takes place
He, The One begins to advise
The beginning of a higher standard
Eternity is the prize

Power lies in the sharing of knowledge
Inferring that we all have ties
Timeless is that of our existence
Eternity is the prize
Gain truth and knowledge
Realize yeast ye dies
Eternity is the prize

All never works out to your advantage
Does this do they surmise
Knowingly or unknowingly do thee revise
Failure in life thus can be expected
Remain to keep yon eyes
All works according to plan
Come soon day of reprise
Eternity is the prize

Continue seeking and exploring to infinity
Eternity is the prize
Freedom gives way to where adventure does wait
Eternity is the prize
Spiritual beliefs soon began to change
Eternity is the prize
Hope to stay spiritually friendly
Eternity is the prize

Eternity is the prize
Eternity is the prize

Having of a Vision or Dreaming

Act III

Fallen upon me, a dream or vision, a key or plea
Having ample reverence and trepidation
On this table I lay, lady in white, standing on right
"Tested positive," I heard, "screamed in my mind"
"Tis Aspera you have," take heed, "Cried in my mind"
As though wind

Those who spend for business or personal
Miserly gathering or thrifty spending a fastidious chore
Dare I call this a vision, one's delusion in mind
For it feeling less painful this dream, a psychotic belief in mind
Hope with faith of wind

When it comes to inheritance of harvest then sow
All should tend to be cautious and conservative of thee superior
All thy mansions go hand and hand with thee investor
Through which door shall one pass, happens in mind
Known must be to all enactment made, begin in mind
Faithfull hoping for wind

Limits of debts are stretched when should be avoided
Unwise have been the choices of those who risk security
Unexpected are they to cost if failed to prepare
Having yet unknown, this a vision or a dream
Invariable squalling of mind
An unsettled consequence of mind
Faithfully hoping for wind

Traveling much distance, many sights did behold
These vision maybe dreams had been foretold
Favor is given to those whom are prepared
Extravagant spending on thee partner whom have not averted
Bringing to thee his articulating light
Appearing to some as sunlight
Hope with faith of wind

Wealth comes from the motivations of all
Determined by the individual desire of one's will
Lifestyle is determined by the power of freedom
Each and every one consider thy morality
Every and each all consider thy liberty
Hope with faith of wind

Backing firing on those whom consistently cut corners
Higher are the gains in His, the belief of his calculated risk
Yielding all, The One in one accord
Vision given to the mind
Uniting all a dream to the mind
Faithfully hoping in wind

Reaching yet again another known but unknown destination
Reviled as ostensibly to be a passageway to thee Creation
Given to this messenger at the gate
See all that is to survey
Yes, go bring them halfway
Faithfully hoping in wind

Organizations and clubs affect the lives of many
Failing will be for all lacking humanity
Monumental changes catalyst is that of cooperation
Meandering through vastness of my mind
Considering the possible nothingness of my mind
Hope with faith of wind

Good intentions are replaced by the egos of some
Failing are these, who feed off society
Whom of which type shall thy decide to join
Threads feed into the mind
Trust in the nourishment in the mind
Hope with faith of wind

All those stay ambitious in discipline of Law
Always continue working strong in responsibility
Knowledge of humanitarianism is love of freedom
Forthcoming still yet to come in my mind
Vision or dreams still yet emerging in mind
Hope with faith of wind

Every One of Ye

Act IV

Introducing new trends shall be thee intent
Planning has gone in to what most do not realize
Glamour is the task maker of thee environment
Spilling forth many who ye criticize
A Love of humanity this lesson is meant
More active involvement in family ties
In deed ye all who fail to listen
Lacking will causes loss in perception
Impulsively bestowing your gifts as tithes
May ye all come to regret ye decision
For ye determination in material advancement
Results from ye disorganized thinking
Thee underprivileged ye see's ye a champion
Expressing thoughts quickly over talking and conniving
Gracious and tactful are ye emotions in controlling
By ye inventing new electronic collaborations
Endure ye towards more positive pursuits
Patience with perseverance brings about much rejection ye
Realistic plans better served by education ye implanting
All ye who disdain conflict likewise
Problems by exaggerations ye
Decisions leading to conflicts surely to be unfurled
Spilling forth in this conflict ye has arisen
Rivalries among many of ye have swirled
Darkness dominating ye has will to win
Yet ye nations shall become combative
What future legacy shall ye persist?
Ye who wants to save the world?

Ode to every one of Ye
Vainly to thee I plea
Let not all ye fail to see

Learning to Love

Act V

Learning to love
Understanding its power and influence
One sets out to rule the macrocosm
The mind working precision in its allegiance
Yet evolving in its vehemence

Requires gaining knowledge
Hoping wishes comes true
Protected yourself, be realistic yet compassionate
As to whether it leaves you blue
Desire your knowledge in spirituality that's true

By being a student of many subjects
Information is eagerly gathered
While inspiring others to do the same
Self realization is a non material in gain
A new philosophy to all is what's to fame

One's heart begins to learn
Success is crucial in its planning
Putting one's own ideas into immediate action
A loss in hard efforts, if goals are not made the for long term
Weathering through these storms is to save and to stay firm

As a result of ones effort
Patience an old yet tried and true method
Running peoples lives maybe the manifestation
Yet, relationships are always in alteration

Remember remolding continually takes place
Gains made in partnerships are gifts of grace
Strong and positively omnipotent is this emotion
When it is the object of the One's devotion

Loving to learn
Arguments do cause snap decisions
Plan thoroughly before one's minds are made up
Explaining all details from beginning middle and end
Relationships then remain positive for minds to transcend

People can and will be convinced of almost anything
By continuing to stretch budgets for luxury items
Make realistic choices by listening to the pros and cons
Submitting only to significant insights and contributions

Loving leaders learn to set examples
Projects and plan should always include others
Never always rely on one's own ability and opinions over others
Discontent always emerges from being forced to follow others

Path to happiness comes by avoiding temper tantrums
Avoid spending extravagantly and long states of depression
Being sure of oneself some will not listen due to emotions
Learn to love the One Heavenly Father's Devotions

Good Is

Good is a bleak house precipitating decisive action, passive aggressively exploring the underworld mining and recycling illusions of strength from sexual excitement. Creating sudden electrical fires in victims of violence spurs defensive feelings in theses freedom fighters. Originality in action displays hidden wealth, buried in matter of the dutiful mother's enormous power. The need for structure and permanence learned with lessons in the home.... cautious behavior when putting ideals into practice, fighting on the behalf of the underdog. Revolutionary are the fireworks of these controlled responses.

Good is valuing the freedom of life's intense emotional unconventional relationships. Free love's domestic crisis of buried feelings manifests emotional blackmail. Unusual is the appearance of the powerful mother's magnetic attractions that transform these feelings. The loving hearts malleability in honest feeling of self love, it is important, in regards to relationships and its popularity towards the pursuit of peace.

Good is the power of language. The secret information....words can kill. Research the poison pen with society's dark thoughts sabotaging through communication. Lesson for survival, fear of change or fear of annihilation is rebels in control use of power, obsessed with order, sabotaging authority by breaking with tradition.

Good is sibling rivalry's radical non-rational mind's idealization of facts. Distorted information is a rebel's quick thinking, reforming anarchist ways to undermine opinions, by being innovative and revolutionary. Meeting resistance when it comes to the importance of truths, insistence does these, large-hearted, self-enlarged, opportunist with big goals on controlling freedom and independence. The explorer infiltrating the mind of the collective asserts incisive communication. Identifying with God's inspiring words, knowledge is power. Quester of visionary competitive mind creates composition by putting thoughts into action. Pride is the uniqueness ones own originality.

Union

Act VII

Saviors in need of the ideal home
Fear of fighting for or against authority
Fear of competition exaggerates behavior
to ye suffering elusive feelings
Emotional drowning of idealized mother
Obsession with self, mother is the victim
Dominations of stamina's endurance
Hard labor, heavy metal, money and power
Father as the victim, lost ego
Expansive are feelings of valuing women
Defining one's ideas in a relationship crisis
The good life is glamorizing self
Characters personality of self-deception
Language barriers to negative thinking
Escaping from self mediumship

Identifying with the victim of the Savior
Pride in compassions importance of vision
Hides true self importance of power Sensitivity
Powerful the fathers transforming pride
For lovers of peace the voice of authority
Compulsive affections are
Tests of strength and courage
Co-operative behavior sensitivity to fairness
The beautiful home of the loving mother
The disciplined mind, learns the hard way
The need to protect, the need for faith.
The mother church, beauty and power
Wants/Needs, Future/Past, Mother/father
Wealth of expansive feelings
Valuing the meaning of

Illuminating taboos of sexual control Transforming appearance The power of love.. Pleasure is God

Regardless of

Act VIII

Injury involving interference
Hurting heeds handicaps
Piques paying attention preventative

Act VIIII

Solitary sentiments of study
Collectible cerebrations conceived
Merited mentations moot

Thee

The romantic adventurer set out to see
Idealized beauty in search oversea
Fairy tale romance to designee
Clandestine relationships by His decree
Putting energy into beauty is vanity
Love and competition of the bourgeoisie
Fighting for money forever will disagree
Assertion and compromise another false plea
Love of dreaming yes could be
Sexual love has no guarantee
Sexual feelers lead a killer bee
Seductions doors skeletons key
Romantic triangles referee
Romantic loves repartee
Beautiful music to sticktight flea
Rebellious feelings to a tolerable degree
Emotional independence singletary pea
The need for space all part of si
Inconsistent behavior be mortars of debris
Changing moods of expected trainee
Fear of losing control to which trustee
Sudden moves comes vendee
Escaping responsibility by those who flee
Undermining authority Yea! Whoopee!
Culture shock banshee
Guilt and reparations to payee
Transcending boundaries of life's admission fee
Lessons of purification and refinements telegraphs, the key
Idealizations of authority, one soul to Thee

Souls

Instincts of good judgment
Focusing on artistic pursuits
Seeking balance and harmony

Sex weakens the will
Understanding power
Brotherly love concept

War with-in the self.
The Father fighting
Winning in pride

Importance of daring,
Keeps focus

Importance of courage
Turns in new directions

Restlessness and recklessness
Loyal and faithful
Be careful whom you love

Discipline aids in achieving goals
Construction determines unexpected changes
Energy needs to retreat

Thirst for higher learning
Fight harder to maintain
Tests of faith

Philosophy of materialism
Definitions of wealth
Large the super ego

Sharing with others in need
Big dreams
Or, grandiose fantasies

Mystical the experience
Great is the escape
Flight of the spiritual

Explorers see
Learning what is truly valued
Life enduring positive pursuits

All

All who want to save the world be sympathetic
Learn to understanding the etheric vibrations
Transforms by appealing directly to emotions
Of entire humanity's utilizing high ideals of wisdom and imagination
Gravitating away from emotional hurts
Excludes causes of ones own unhappiness
The exceptional creative gain in sagacity
His self realization to the meaning of life
Eternity's home and variety of wide activities
Redemptions looking to a higher greater plane

Epilogue

CLARIFYING LIFE UNDERSTANDING OF
EVERLASTING SPIRITUAL TRUTH

Clarifying

Do you feel something in the air in needing of care
You and your arrogance in due of its diligence
Wanting no Czar believing in thee do compare

What he will not allow seeing judgments run ye ambivalence
Against the peoples will surely some may kill
Radicals and rebels hears sagacity's intent with minds equivalence

Taking your lumps means to stimulate the will
The act of repealing as to make a decision
What was one is now two comprehends the bill

The summoning of the three all commanding of vision
The circling of vultures awaiting the degrade
An arming of a People all unleashed to envision

The crusade being much more than just mere blade
Our outrage grows towards an inevitable upheaval
A cry for humanity in hopes hard to dissuade

Fore humanities fall far back before medieval
And option there yet may if only all could see
There is a coming of a season longed in retrieval

The line in the sand drawn at liberty's tree
The crying voice wails alone in the dark
Says you hold the key in parting the red sea

All words of attest scream the words by a lark
A time of change comes this eon
The steering of the course takes control of the ark

Of histories repeat unit thee plebeian
The multiplying of the free all numerous He diversity
Brings winds of change thoughts do thy protean

For civility's rebirth altogether quest internally
An ode to the people whom now are aware

Life's

The heart, grand encompassing when used in animation
Father and child, embracing once utilized internal causation
Thus fallen, arise unseen power to thee vitality
An ode to you, acquire exponent in he spirituality

Truths gift, unexpended he is in spirit
My velvet stain, remaining in me to here it
Your will, certified by way of construction
Missing you, evident inward course to destruction

In friendship, relative to the transactions one accounts
Even fear, congenator in dealing nonpareil surmounts
Going into the night, as comparative is thy lurking
A man's, testament proportionally in the reworking

Unbridled passion, electricity's effectiveness in liveliness
Poetry, movement's effectualness for timelessness
I desire so, forward motion for its formulation
Feelings of love, headfirst activity's most used orchestration

Trusting, ontogeny from within contents
Possession by her love, exploitations passim misrepresents
A Son's hug, a maturation of deeds in one's reflection
Smiles of a Daughter, evolution of seed in one's affection

A child, loading questions of biography
A truth of love, burdening gestures to crystallography
The unseen cut, payloads of interrogation do rupture
Being forced, consignment in gesticulations of structure

Why wait for, the end of one's existence
I speak in a tongue, for the oddment in persistence
Knowing of its peculiarity absolute
Features of the heart, in its rarity resolute

Are life's tips these be they

Understanding of

Desires and wills cognitive oneness in supplication
The paths and the planks condition wholeness an option
Sighting rationalities integrity one explanation
Requires thoughts of He thee main adoption

Honoring the one with comprehensive resolve
Stating what union of discernment one must have engagement
The enigma exchange leads one to evolve
Despots all promise battle continuous of two in enragement

Clicks inclination from the start
The pain and joy of sex is characterized in lies by devise
The coming of brighter day's empathy thus impart
Between the darkness and the light is personification's demise or prize

The power of belief the death of a thief
Liberty is wills understanding

Everlasting

Is thee Past, Present and Future

The blue marbles' arrant revolution
Inspiration at its best
Flawed yet I stand goddamn

Knocking and asking prayer unceasing
The roaring of a Lune gross
Yielding light consummate

The Repealing of an act leads to fact
The pattern is double-dyed
Undoing, unending

Wishes thoroughgoing live controlling
Work on gaining perfection
Regenerating blame

Mental explorations extremely deuced
Balance continually
Health be eternally

Creativity gives way to staring
Home immortal his portal
Intelligently see

Communicating infernal torment
His everlasting flower
Yours is the choice to make

Me mind aeonian subconscious belong
Myself permanent distress
I am blessed to be sure

You stark an aliment one and together
For all need to be complete
The Poetry of Soup

Spiritual

Join no longer deny uncertainty of thee
Emissary who died for all, your
Savior who stood
Ultimately for all
Sacrificing along with his blood
For universal and harmonious
Omnipotent all encompassing never ending forever bending
Revolving life-force that is the secret
Those who seek to know
Heavenly Father's whose life giving
Etheric vibrations are infinities
Eternal life giving power thusly so
Who through all thoughts one may propagate
He that is among the unworldly
Only death can be found earthly
Worship in regards to all sacred matters
Always being in concern matters of its affecting
Never quit gaining incorporeal
They who watch come to see
Love who is I am
I am is who Love is
Forever He is everlasting
Embracing you who is I am
Dry Landers reap the fields they seed
Irrigators nourish those fields that originate
Evokers ignite that which is in need to endure
Zephyrs forge performing in function

Truths

All
Soul for
Thee
Regardless of
Union
God says
Good is
Learning to love
Everyone one of Ye
Having of a vision or dreaming
Eternity's prize
Righteous
Enunciated
Inscribers
Now and forever

Resources

www.thosewhoseektoknow.com